50 Percent Love

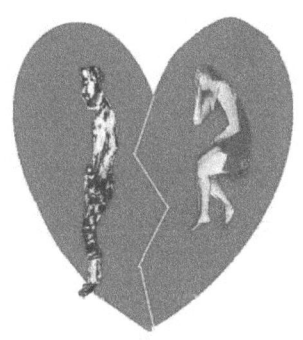

Gloria Duran

©2020

Table of Contents

LOVE 4
Unreturned Love 5
Recollection 6
Epitaph for Donald Trump 7
Post Mortem 8
Rebellious Larynx 9
Dirge for Sasha 10
Manolo 11
Wandering 12
On Love 13
After Reading Too Much Dorothy Parker 14
Subterranean Current 15
For Anita 16
Triolet 17
NATURE 18
Gatekeeper 19
Open Windows 21
Elegy to Cold September, 1951 22
Spring Twilight 23
Seize the Night 25
Rainy Night 26

Winter Landscape 27
Cushioned Night..29
   TIME..30
Two-Story Landscape 31
Dominus 32
Dust Veil 33
Emptiness..34
Time...35
Glance at Tepotzlan 37
Looking 39
   WAR 40
Poseidon's Fields (1940)..41
Autumn, 1939 (After start of World War II).....................43
Eastern Europe, 1939 (For Dance or Mime) 45
   YOUTH...48
The Barefoot Boy with Shoes On 49
World Spoon 50
Why Do Babies Cry?..51
Coming of Age 52
   ADVENTURE 53
Mexico Again...54
A Trip by Train to Bangor, Maine 56
Macmillan's Song (For the Arctic Explorer).....................58

LOVE

Unreturned Love

Ah, never will you guess,
my dear,
the hours I dream of you
and hold you near,
year after year,
and write these verses too.
And never shall you
hear my heart
that wails
like crying skies—
united from
two realms apart
when you're before my eyes.

Nor ever will my love
be earned
by anyone but you,
and as it will
not be returned,
'twill perish when I do.
Oh fool to love,
unloved, I know,
the cruelest jest of fate!
No, never would I have it so,
but now
it is too late.

And so my heart is never free
for one whose love I've earned
unconsciously, and e'er must be,
like mine,
quite un-returned.

Recollection

It was a sweet-breathed autumn day,
a fragrant, fragile thing,
a moment that had lost its way
from a girlish, care-free Spring.

Oh this, a transient, glowing dart
that pierced with sudden pain,
the inner recess of my heart
for it could not remain.

But as I drank the dew-kissed air
and said it could not be,
suddenly I saw you there
and smiling, too, at me!

It only happens once—
a wing—
dropped from the gracious sky,
a misplaced, adolescent Spring
which cannot ever die.

Epitaph for Donald Trump

You must have been a wayward lad,
a villain amd an adolescent cad
You must have had the wrong intentions
and other things I need not mention.
I swear you're someone to deplore,
but still you never were a bore!

You must have been a born seducer,
your morals could not be much looser.
In fact, as far as I may search you,
I find you are without a virtue,
Except as I have said before,
"At least you never were a bore!"

Post Mortem

I cannot say that I would love them
after what they meant for me;
Nor can I say I'm jealous of them
though, doubtless, I should be.
But also they cause me no pity
for while it lasts,
Their lives are pretty.
I merely wish that they were dead,
His loves who've followed in my stead.

Rebellious Larynx

Why is that with other men
my tongue slides nimbly as my pen?
And since I've known that we were through,
I've dreamt of things to say to you,
But when, non prevenu, we meet,
I can be neither cruel nor sweet?
I choke on words, my throat grows dry,
my tonsils stretch; I wonder why
I lack my knack of repartee.
Why is there nothing I can say?
I've broken loose from Cupid's fetter,
or does my larynx know me better?

Dirge for Sasha

Gold as the oak leaves in October,
soft as a tassel of late-summer corn,
You were the part of me that was wild and free;
When I was with you, I was new-born.
Nature was magic, all love and surprise,
but who loves the master after his dog dies?

Now it is autumn, or so people say,
but you were *my* autumn, and you've gone away,
leaving the oak leaves as cracked, brown November,
leaving me old and afraid to remember,
draining the forest from scarlet to gray—
Nature was magic, all love and surprise,
but who loves the master after her dog dies?

Winter is coming to make up your bed,
crystals of silver you once loved to tread,
You were the part of me that was wild and free,
the part of me that lies with you—dead.
Nature was magic, all love and surprise,
but who loves a master after his dog dies?

Manolo

We've a Friendship
that will never end
It's a tree
that will never fall
but will sway and bend.
And the sap of the tree
can be weak or strong
just as the wind whistles,
or howls,
its own secret song.

*Love is my foe,
all this I know,
the tree of love
will always win:
for it knows not how to end
but only
how to begin.*

Wandering

Beneath my window, lovers sigh,
The night is soft and dark,
My heart takes quiet leave of me
to wander in the park;
Wandering in the park, am I—
my hand in someone else's hand,
But now my heart goes happily
to where I used to stand.

On Love

Do I love you
or do I only think I do?
But how can there be
certainty
that what they call love
is love,
or what I see as you
is you?
Perhaps, it isn't true!
Perhaps, I do not love you
because there is no you,
nor I,
nor love,
but only we,
the particles of dust,
fumbling in space,
consumed by lust,
reaching for a hold—
a resting placc.

After Reading Too Much Dorothy Parker

I have a poem for all my lads,
so why not one for you?
You'll join the old anthology;
Yes, that is what you'll do.

You will depart from in my heart,
and languish here instead.
And pleasant company you'll keep
with Bill, and Jack and Ned.

You need not think you're different, sir,
or better than the rest!
Nor think I'll nurse you longer than
a cold within my chest.

I'll simply write your epitaph
and toss you here inside,
"Here lies a rather pleasant lad,
But, then, he always lied."

Subterranean Current

My love sits and writes poems
to the houses and the fountains
and the distant mountains.
In my heart, too, there are poems
to my youth
that flies through my fingers
like fountain spume.
Poems to my other loves
reflected now in swift flowing water,
tender eyes, a smile, a whispered word-
No more. The current
sweeps away the vision.
Poems. Hundreds of poems.
My heart is bursting with fullness
A fountain of memories
spouts inside me.
It presses against my rib-cage,
tightens my throat.
My tongue is frozen
with unspoken cri*es.*
They strain for an outlet
in poems, in a gateway to eternity,
but finding none
they disconnect and die.

For Anita

Without you, I find no precious stones
Or pink shells buried in the sand
Nor hear the scraping of waves that sound
their ardent greeting as they reach land.
Without you, I see no more fiery sunsets
Behind the tall, slim silhouettes
of swaying, wind-bent grass
Nor the paper-thin egrets
Which come to us as we pass.
Without you, the world has become less magic
Your Iranian bowl is lost on the shore
The Arabian nights are now only tragic.
We hear their seductive calls no more.

Triolet

Last night I saw you in my dreams,
though still we were apart,
and tripling lightly o'er moonbeams
last night I saw you in my dreams.
But like before in life it seems
You tiptoed through my heart;
Last night I saw you in my dreams,
though we were still apart.

NATURE

Gatekeeper

He's the gatekeeper
in the condo's pool,
you won't question
his authority
if you value your eyes.
He's the St. Peter
of our little
Florida paradise.
Although he stands
Only four feet high,
his cutting edge is lethal,
especially,
if you're a fish.

Some people
call him a blue heron,
but this is all that I can say:
he is basically grey
with a very pale, bluish, streak
in the middle of his face
leading down
to his menacing beak.

I swim a prudent distance
from our gatekeeper.
I seek to unobtrusively
examine that beak.
Not to make him
take offense, you see.
Though he doesn't seem
to be watching me.

What's chilling **about** him
is that neck—

so thick, so white so long
so serpent-like.

When he senses danger,
that neck coils down,
preparing to attack.

I wonder—
what does the gatekeeper
ponder
other than the skeletal remains
of the fish
he scatters at our pool's side?

During his long periods
of immobility,
which thoughts
cross his mind?
Does he know I am studying him?
Does he consider me?
Is he wondering about
all the same things that I do,
the mysteries of our earth and sky and sea?
Could he know any of the answers?

Open Windows

Open windows beckon the Spring
And call for the world to step in
my heart.
There are echoes of shouts in the streets,
children's voices and sounds far away.

Only chimneys stand apart,
Silent, cold, grey
Like tombstones of cities long dead,
Cutting their edges against a pale sky.

Theirs are the sharpness that touches my heart
and the voices of Spring lose their way.

Elegy to Cold September, 1951

Amber petals decomposing on my window-sill,
Plaintive tremor of a leaf.
Sudden chill like early coming of a dreaded guest
Still-born Spring is buried in autumnal grief—
Wrap my coat around me closer still
All the warmth of life has gone.
Spring came not and summer stayed away.
Why, then, do I linger on?

Spring Twilight

If you had seen me
You would say I walked.
How little you'd suspect
I had no feet
nor legs, nor arms nor anything
but air.
I flowed,
gently, softly,
lasciviously,
bathing my pale pink nothingness
in the warm, impalpable sea
of moon-lit, sun-lit space.
I drowned
silently, painlessly
in the twilight,
on the country road
buried 'neath rosy atoms of light
where even the shadows of trees
held their breath
in a world of fireflies
bursting into life,
phosphorescent, shimmering green—
a sub-oceanic garden
of jewelry blossoms
that sparkle and disappear.
Somewhere, somehow
street-lamps glowed
a timid, apple-green:

A shade paler than the fireflies.
And I came to your door
Re-embodied. But I had flown
I had not walked.

Seize the Night

Clouds of day linger tonight,
Flimsy wraiths which haunt pale sky,
Smoke dressed in the opaque light
of a newborn moon nearby.
Never was a sight like this,
wine to lovers, poet's praise.
What a night to reminisce
and to wish for other days.

Rainy Night

Twisting waters
bathed in mist
muffled, hushed;
the current drowned.
drowned in night
and raindrops' breath,
mixed with willows
whispered sounds,
willows with their finger tips
water-laden,
cool and tender
on my lips.
Lamplight veiled
in cushioned night.
Milky diamonds
fill my eyes,
flicker dimly on the stones
tip toe, sadly, through the grass
as in search
of other nights.

Winter Landscape

Once I was a fan dancer, too.
Once, a green summer ago
my love came and said
"I adore you,
I would rest in your shade forever."

But I did not know
he said that to all the trees.
Still he was not untrue.
For we were all the same,
voluptuous, green,
swaying to passionate winds
and even to gentle breezes
so he did not know me
from any of the others.

But soon autumn came
to tear away the fans,
and I was glad and said,
"Now he can see the charms
of my clean and naked
skeleton."
So I stretched out
my loving, shade-less arms,

But now he noticed me no more.

Instead,
he closed his eyes,
shivered in the cold,
and like an old man
who accidently
sees himself in a mirror,
he quickly turned away,
painfully limped all the way home
and shut tight
his broken cottage door.

Cushioned Night

Twisting waters
Bathed in mist
Muffled, hushed,
The current drowned.
Drowned in night
And raindrops' breath,
Mixed with willows
Whispered sounds,
Willows with their finger tips
Water-laden,
Cool and tender
On my lips.
Lamplight veiled
In cushioned night.
Milky diamonds
Fill my eyes
Flicker dimly on the stones
Tip toe sadly through the grass
As in search
Of other nights.

TIME

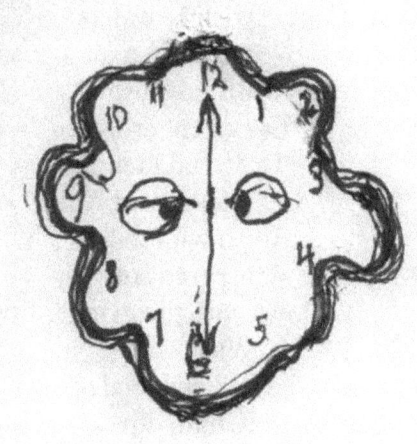

30

Two-Story Landscape

I see a row of buildings
shedding their plaster
as worn-out shells.
A red door
is blackened with age,
and slumps dejectedly
on its last hinge.
There is a bicycle repair shop
and a thin dog stretched out
brushing away flies.
While above me,
by two-stories height-
an artist looks from his cracked window,
smiles, and paints a final stroke
on his vision
of a tropical night.

Dominus

He comes not in
golden chariots
that sweep through fleecy air.
And no trumpeters announce him
in an ostentatious flair.
He is rather in the sun beams,
and He comes to us in sweet dreams
that we dream in foolish innocence,
not knowing He is there.

Dust Veil

There is a thin veil of dust
on the floor, on the window sills—
Impersonal reminder of earth and time
recorded in particles of matter
laid down at the standard rate
of deposition.

But in my heart,
hours and days forget to come
or time enters at a different rate of speed.
Pain kindled weeks ago burns bright,
leaps up in searing glory
at a word, a cry
and glares in sightless accusation
at the dust-veiled room.

Emptiness

Emptiness has many faces:
the face of repose of an empty house
waiting to be filled by love.
It is a comfortable face
of sofas and soft pillows
which caress me visually.
And I say,
"Yes, I must have you reupholstered.
He is wearing you thin
in one place,"

But there are other vacant forms
whose faces I've grown to hate.
The emptiness of thin chairs
which retreat into wallpaper,
who caresses not, nor are caressed,
but only wait
for nothing to happen;
For no one to come.
They hold their vacant laps—
vacant for all eternity,
this is the emptiness
of the vacant face
that creeps inside me.

Time

Tick, tick, tick
Three thirty, four o' clock,
soon it will be five.
My dear, you wish your life away,
counting the hours.
You cannot live at all that way.
Since today is the future of yesterday
And tomorrow
tomorrow is only today.

Tick, tick,
No, you must not watch that clock
heartlessly, soullessly counting your days.
Each tick
and a lifetime is gone.
How can you sit there and wait?
You will never hear this minute again
Live it before it's too late,
Live it with love or with hate
But live it!
Tick,
It is gone
gone like the rest
to the sunless, shadow-less world
of unspent time.
Oh my child, what is wrong?
Do you know? No?

Tick, tick
Is it life? This is life.
Is it love? Do you dream

of a gallant young knight on his horse?
Then go seek him while there is still light
in your eyes.
For the darkness and night
are your foes.

Tick, tick, tick,
The world is spinning
outside your window.
Yet you sit
And watch by the pane,
like Elaine in her glass
watch life pass, watch it pass
and it's gone.

Glance at Tepotzlan

Down from the gold of Aztec cliffs,
part clay, part tile, part verdant palms,
it slumbers in a wondrous sleep,
lost to the world in buried charms.

Lost with the glory of Ancient Spain
that cries its tale in a hollow knell,
from the spires of a crumbled, blood-built church—
and the mouth of a cracked and time-worn bell.

Here is its story emblazoned in the land,
unconquered by time, untouched by men's lust,
as free as its people who still dare to stand
while temple and convent both bow down to dust.

Dream for a moment into its dim past,
into the splendor that never shall cease
in its bright people, the poets of old,
into its enchanted and slumbering peace.

See this bronze peon in strange Aztec dress
kneel in his temple of jade and of gold,
and see him at prayer in the church once again.
It is the same man you behold!

His masters' clay glories surrender+ to God
and return to the earth whence they came.
But the gold corn comes up, and the bronze man
comes up

every year after year just the same.

Reborn with the ages, he sprouts with his crops,
so old that all time disappears,
and the man and the earth are immortal alike,
unblemished by centuries' tears.

Behold now his land with the tassels of silk
and its story in crumbling clay,
too bright for a dream, too strong for a thought,
one glance and we look away.

Looking

From the valley I look upward,
From the mountain
I look down,
But whatever it is I'm looking for
Is nowhere to be found.
If I found it,
Would I know it?
Would I know the false from true?
But I'll just keep on looking,
Looking, looking, looking
Until it comes to view.
And I think I'll never find it,
And perhaps I shouldn't try,
But I know I'll keep on looking
'til the moment that I die.

WAR

Poseidon's Fields (1940)

Poseidon's fields are rich this year
with bodies of the valiant dead,
who find their watery tombs so still
below the rumble overhead;
And so a million heroes sleep
beneath a blanket wet and deep
that covers all the sea god's bed.

Oh, unawares, you cross their graves
where Neptune's verdant jungles grow
on every sea where wars were fought
in each unfathomed inch men know
we trample on our brother's head
and see no drop of blood he shed
to mark his sepulcher below.

Beneath the depths he lies in peace
for him there is no war today.
He need not man the sunken ship
or drive the deadly mine away
Headless of battle, time or tide,
headless that foes sleep side by side
they lie embraced, the blue and grey.

The waves have swallowed up their cares.
What matters now: the flag or land?
or ship that rusts and turns to moss
in mockery of human hand?
That earth and sky that God has made

       is never won by human blade
the conquerors dead must understand.

For them the futile strife is gone,
the sound of bombs, the cannon roar,
and blasphemies on God-made throats
like greed and hate, exist no more;
At rest, the valiant heroes sleep
beneath a blanket wet and deep
that guards their peace forevermore.

Autumn, 1939 (After start of World War II)

Where are the green leaves of past yesterdays,
myriad spirits that inhabit each bough
clad in their mantels, a glowing array.
Where is their green luster now?

Where are those jewels that I saw last night
set in a black velvet case?
Who is the thief that has drawn them from sight?
And left a grey sky in their place?

What has become of the fairy-like gleam
now that magic has gone?
Surely it was but a wonderful dream
to be dispelled by the dawn?

Where are those visages that we still love,
glowing in youth's bright array?
Smiling unseen from their haven above,
just as those leaves blown away?

Gone with tempest, usurped by the cold,
these are the vandals of yore;
And as I dream back, oh was it not told
that such dread things were no more?

Where is this stillness that never could be,

even as absence of breeze?
Who, then, can issue so strong a decree
that it is obeyed by the trees?

Where is the pen that can make life stand still
just in the pose that we love?
None that its wielded by sword-stained hand will,
Even in peace-maker's glove.

Where is the rest that we never shall find
In a world that will always be strange?
Like those bright faces and leaves left behind,
buried in two season's change?

Eastern Europe, 1939 (For Dance or Mime)

I cannot talk,
I dare not speak,
Someone may hear!
The walls have ears.
You know we're watched
both night and day
by eyes of "friends"
whose lips betray.
But we are free in a new order
Of frightening things,
Free to worship our powerful lord.
Free as his echo
that rings and rings.
Free! Yes, free as the galley slave,
who sweats for the greater glory
of Rome or Spain,
free to bow down
at our new Caesar's feet
and to writhe
in a conquered nation's shame.

Oh the winds and the thunder and storms were an omen,
and the far-off shouts and the passing of day,
but the worst one was the closest
the omen of fear and of freedom's decay.
But wait, be still and listen.

In the smoldering ash I find a spark
that flickers despite its shackles,
that whispers a dawn from the dark
with light that is only reflection,
but grows with the fanning of breath
to stir each slumbering flame to action
from out of the ashes of death.

Now sparks leap out in each little prison
of this whole ugly structure aflame
and reeking with its kindling blood
like death behind life's name.
See it shiver and sputter and tremor
as it quivers at its own device.
See it fall with a shriek in its own red-hot flames,
but remember its spectacle's price.
Yes, remember my son, in your freedom
that rises from blood-heated strife,
Remember, remember your fathers had lost it
and paid to regain it with life.
But it rises from centuries' ashes,
rises slowly with youth's growing pain,
rises, rises from ashes
to a world that was nursed on its name,
to a world where men talk
who've forgotten the fear
of malevolent eyes
or an enemy's ear,
to a world that can laugh,
that can shout to the skies,
that has scrubbed all the black
from a hundred white lies,

to a world where men dance,
and not march and not bow
where you sing and shout
for this day that is now.

YOUTH

The Barefoot Boy with Shoes On

The barefoot boy with shoes on
was lifting up his feet,
and thinking 'bout the days
when he'd had a slimmer seat,

'Bout streams still unpolluted,
the ones not polluted by him,
of certain things he might have done,
of the man he might've been.

Oh, the barefoot boy with shoes on
in nineteen ninety one,
can't understand why in this land
it's harder to have fun.

What happened to that quiet stream
where he fished as a kid?
while grown up people ran the world—
or else, he thought they did.

But now that hate is in the air
like sparrows on the wing,
he wonders what those grownups did
or had they done a thing?

Or were the rest all barefoot boys
a-snoozing by their streams,
that ran from blue to black to red
while everybody dreamed?

World Spoon

Her tongue was sweetly glazed with plums
    emptied from the purplish bowl,
But she held the dish in her baby hands
    and she drank it eyes and soul.
"See mother, see the dark, dark juice
    like the night without a moon;
I always save the juice for last,
    so's the world is in my spoon."

Why Do Babies Cry?

When I hear a baby cry
I often wonder why
And this is what it seems to me:
He must appear
From a distant sphere
Where it's much better to be.

Then if he complains
In a wailing voice
We need to understand
He was wrenched away
Without much choice
Of where he was to land.

So as I look out
On this fertile ground
Where the babies multiply,
I remember that
I once made that sound
And I cry, and cry, and cry.

Coming of Age

It was fun being children together,
in a world of old women and men,
like the friendship of broth and sister
that I hope we can discover again.

It is only three months that we left it
over three thousand miles and deep sea,
and the time and the tide have flowed rapidly on.
Do you think that now it can still be?

We were bound by the friendship of travel
and we clung to it, held to it fast
in a dream of bright, far-away places
but at home do you think it can last?

I remember those winding strange markets
where we bargained for blankets and lace,
and I see you with flickering shadows
that a Spanish hearth casts on your face.

We were fanciful, light-hearted children,
Oh, but can we be that once again?
For the world is no longer a dreamland,
and we are the women and men.

ADVENTURE

Mexico Again

This is a land
Where I would not have wished to die
But even now
Death clings to my side
In parched deserts
And purple mountains
Just as someone else
Someone centuries before me
walks behind me
Faces me in every recess
With a face that is empty and featureless.

I cannot cast out this shadow
Who clutches my heart, my breath
Seals me on the train of centuries,
Curtains drawn,
No stop.
This is everlasting death.
Oh let me jump from the window
I stand alone in the aisle
Cut out from the sun,
The music and laughter.
Even tears here are hushed,
Choked before they rise
Drowned in an ancient well
That is dry.

This is a land eternal
Enshrined to the dead

This is Olympus
Of bright sunsets
Of shrines clutched to the breast
Of mountains
Here there is life of the Gods
Life majestic
Life of volcanoes
Fiery, bright,
Nursed by the heavens,
By rainbows,
Lips of volcanoes
Pressed to voluptuous clouds
Clouds that cascade
Down the mountains
To drink of the foam of the sea.
But for me…
who passes through desert
There is no life,
Only dreams of life far away,
Of simple, quiets lands,
Of cool pine-banked streams
Whose source has vanished.
So I gaze at streams in the desert
Knowing they are only mirage.

A Trip by Train to Bangor, Maine

Onward, on and on I travel
Over hill and dale I go
past the river's slow unravel
through a world I scarcely know,
while a raucous engine bellows
in a voice both loud and low.

Now I pass a crimson forest
golden splashed with Autumn's shades,
fairer than those at a florist's
when a dying sunset fades
on Demeter's rainbow laces
that adorn her chestnut braids.

And this rolling meadow, see it
silhouetted against the sky
why, oh must I quickly flee it
as the engine thunders by,
stopping not that I may linger
just a moment, then slip by,

while inside each house I see there
in a person I could love,
yet I know not, nor do I care,
nor do they care for my love.
Thoughtlessly I pass life's treasures
And someone chuckles from above.

But the world grows ever darker.

Silent falls the veil of night,
blanketing each country marker,
sweeping out the grains of light.
Now the earth is but a shadow
that I merge through in swift flight.

Macmillan's Song (For the Arctic Explorer)

Have you ever wished to step across the sands of time and tide,
and to reach a point beyond which real and unknown spheres divide?
There to push aside the sordid real for the infinite of space?
Come then, let me take you by the hand and to that distant place
where the white stars of infinity alone, unknown abide.
We shall sail those icy waters in the north wind's sweeping stride
And will reach his snowy birthplace with all heaven as our guide
to the land of gushing sunlight
to a world where there is no night
And the snows of distant centuries beneath the waters hide.

We shall touch those crystal mountains as they softly, swiftly glide
where the oceans gleam like mirror—
deep and clear and cold and wide
and shall see feel our white sails flying
and the lone white seagulls crying,
crying, crying,
that we hasten with the coming of the tide.

www.ingramcontent.com/pod-product-compliance
Lightning Source LLC
Chambersburg PA
CBHW031510040426
42444CB00024B/1189